SPORTS FOR SPROUTS

SOCCER

Holly Karapetkova

ROURKE PUBLISHING

Vero Beach, Florida 32964

www.rourkepublishing.com

Photo credits: Cover © Rob Marmion; Title Page © Wendy Nero, Crystal Kirk, Leah-Anne Thompson, vnosokin, Gerville Hall, Rob Marmion; Page 3 © Rob Marmion; Page 4 © Rob Marmion; Page 7 © Rob Marmion; Page 8 © Rob Marmion; Page 11 © Rob Marmion; Page 12 © Ricardo Molina; Page 14 © Blue Door Publishing; Page 17 © GeoM; Page 18 © Rob Marmion; Page 21 © Ricardo Molina; Page 22 © Crystal Kirk, Sonya Etchison, GeoM; Page 23 © Robert Pernell, Scott Sanders, Rob Marmion; Sidebar Silhouettes © Sarah Nicholl

Editor: Meg Greve

Cover and page design by Nicola Stratford, Blue Door Publishing

Library of Congress Cataloging-in-Publication Data

Karapetkova, Holly.
  Soccer / Holly Karapetkova.
     p. cm. -- (Sports for sprouts)
  ISBN 978-1-60694-320-5 (hard cover)
  ISBN 978-1-60694-820-0 (soft cover)
  ISBN 978-1-60694-561-2 (bilingual)
  1. Soccer--Juvenile literature. I. Title.
  GV943.25.K37 2009
  796.334--dc22
                                        2009002255

Printed in the USA
CG/CG

www.rourkepublishing.com - rourke@rourkepublishing.com
Post Office Box 643328 Vero Beach, Florida 32964

I play **soccer.**

3

I wear **shin guards** and **cleats**.

I wear a green **uniform**. I am on the green team.

7

I can kick the ball with my feet.

I cannot touch the ball with my hands.

We have girls and boys on our teams.

We kick the ball into the **goal**. We score one point.

The **goalie** tries to stop the ball. He can use his hands or his feet.

17

Sometimes my team wins. Sometimes we lose.

We always have fun!

Glossary

cleats (KLEETS): Cleats are special shoes with spikes on the bottom to keep people from slipping.

goal (GOHL): A goal is the netted space where players try to kick the ball to score points.

goalie (GOHL-ee): The goalie is the player who guards the goal and tries to keep the ball from going in.

soccer (SOK-ur): Soccer is a game played with a ball where each team tries to kick the ball into the other team's goal.

shin guards (SHIN gardz): Shin guards are special stiff pads that protect the legs.

uniform (YOO-nuh-form): A uniform is special clothing worn by all the members of a team.

Index

Websites

About The Author

Holly Karapetkova, Ph.D., loves writing books and poems for kids and adults. She teaches at Marymount University and lives in the Washington, D.C., area with her husband, her son K.J., and her two dogs, Muffy and Attila.